Six Simple Steps to Success Vol. 4

Making Business Connections That Counts

The Gimmick-free Guide to Authentic Online Relationships

with Influencers and Followers

Written and Published By: Michal Stawicki

Your network

is

your net worth

MAKING BUSINESS CONNECTIONS THAT COUNT

TABLE OF CONTENT

FOREWORD BY AARON WALKER PRESIDENT AND FOUNDER OF VIEW FROM THE TOP

The value of most activities in business pales in comparison to the value of making business connections that count. My friend, Michal Stawicki masterfully depicts how to be authentic in a virtual world. To his admission, this was a real struggle just a few years earlier. Overcoming great personal adversities, upper limit challenges, and an extremely introverted personality, Michal preserves and shares here exactly how you can as well.

Following his easy to understand basic principles of forging meaningful relationships with local or global influencers is nothing short of magnificent. Watching, step by step, how Michal unfolds connecting with business people appears to be as natural as most everyday activities that we perform daily. Sharing how vulnerability, transparency and honesty are all beneficial on this quest for connectivity. Michael demonstrates how to have established rapport with new found friendships that will soon be highly leverageable. This is not a one-sided relationship; he teaches how mutually beneficial kindred spirits become, adding creativity, vision and strength to everyone.

When personal objectives are sidelined, and a "win-win" attitude is formulated, magic happens. Michal adds so many interesting tips on how to place your agenda aside for the greater good of the relationship. By doing so, the unforeseen reciprocity is magnified ten-fold. Throughout the book, he lays out a plan of action that is unquestionably undeniable. Michal demonstrates the importance of staying on their radar consistently. This invariably fosters many friendships and business opportunities. Be mindful of passing judgement until all the facts are disclosed, he warns. Follow-up is paramount, and Michal details an easy system that anyone can follow.

My personal favorite is when Michal points out that we have nothing to lose, how so true this is. If we want different results it's incumbent upon us as individuals to change our course of action. Are you having difficulty making connections that count? Follow this grand plan and you will reach heights never before imagined. *Making Business Connections That Count* can transform your life.

1. I'M A VERY UNLIKELY NETWORKER

My qualifications, with respect to networking, are questionable at best. And that's good news for you.

Four years ago I had no business contacts. The reason is simple—I had neither business background nor experience. I'd only been an employee. Utilizing the methods I will show you in this book, I've been able to start and grow my first business to a profitable level. And I've been able to meet a lot of new people, build rapport with them, do business with them, and get their help.

What is more, although you might not guess it now, I was a hardcore introvert three years ago. I couldn't start a conversation with a stranger. It was beyond my capability.

So, if I could build a network of business contacts, I estimate your chances are much higher. Let's take a look at how low my abilities were **in the middle of 2012.**

I was a little frustrated about my life. Everything was OK—my health, my spiritual life, my finances, my career and family—but none of it was great. I had no vision for my life; I was just getting by each day. However, I was in the right mindset to try new things.

I read a book by Jeff Olson, *The Slight Edge*, and something clicked inside me. I decided to move on with my life.

I needed to focus on my finances more. Three years prior, I had been laid off from my job. My family had to dip deeply into our savings. I had a 30-year mortgage to pay and just a few thousand dollars of savings. I did some quick calculations and realized that my IT career was an insufficient vehicle to take me to financial freedom. I needed to start a business.

I had no idea where to start. The entirety of my business experience was a failed attempt at developing a multi-level marketing venture when I was seventeen years old and it wasn't an encouraging memory.

I had no clue what to do. The most successful entrepreneur I knew was my uncle. His company had been running for about 20 years, but it wasn't thriving. Two years previously he had needed to take a short-term bank loan to be able to pay his employees.

In brief, I didn't feel I was qualified to start a brick-and-mortar business. I didn't have the resources for that, either.

I started to look for online opportunities. It took me more than half a year to discover what I wanted to do. I wanted to earn my living through writing.

I had no experience or education in writing. I didn't have an interesting background, idea, or story to tell. I wasn't a celebrity who could sell my story to hundreds of thousands of my fans. I hadn't done anything significant in my life. I hadn't overcome big struggles or attained great successes I could brag about.

I didn't know anyone who self-published their work, and English is not my first language. All in all, my starting level was "below zero." I had nothing to offer. In 2012 my story could serve only as a warning sign: "Don't do what this guy has done." Until that moment in time, I had been wasting my life.

At the beginning of April 2013, I started writing my first book. In the next two and a half years, I published twelve books and sold over 17,000 copies. I attribute much of my success to networking skills. Many successful businessmen say that the core of a business is connections and interactions with people, rather than any business-specific skills or market acumen. I tend to agree with them.

It took seven or eight months before my networking efforts translated into significant monetary reward. But networking is not about monetary rewards; it's about human-to-human connections. The money follows the growth of your network, but if you focus on making money and put it first, growing your network is an uphill struggle. Within the next couple of years I achieved some remarkable results: a rock star with two million followers featured my blog post on Twitter, I connected with online entrepreneurs who have five-, six- and seven-figure businesses, I exchanged emails and tweets with millionaires. I was even on the phone with one!

You probably wonder if I have a secret. Good news for you: there is no secret. There rarely is a "secret sauce" in any business realm. It's quite easy to learn the "hows" of any business; it's the personal implementation that gets tricky. But if you ask me the core of my networking success, I would say simply authenticity and tenacity. I didn't have to do anything fancy to connect with other people. It was enough to just be me. I consistently followed some people over long periods of time and provided value to them. Those two traits are behind my successes, and anyone can apply them. You don't need a book to tell you how to be yourself—you are the world's expert on that!

I have learned some tips and tricks, however, that have improved my results, and that is what I'd like to share with you in this book. If you're not genuine and persistent, these tricks won't help you. But as long as you are being yourself and being consistent, these tips will help push you over the top. Let's dive in!

Remember:

- There rarely is any 'secret sauce' in any business realm.
- You need only authenticity and tenacity to be effective in networking.
- Those are universal human traits and everyone can apply them, including you.

Action Items:

- Reflect. Decide what you think matters most in this world.
- Consider how you could effectively share this belief with others.

2. NETWORKING IS MUCH EASIER THAN YOU THINK

What really hinders you in any unfamiliar area is your mindset. When you encounter new information, you always ask: *"Is it true? Is it possible?"* The story I presented in the first chapter is 100% true. As it proves, it's possible. Your initial hesitancy to believe new things is just a filter in your brain protecting you against rushing into a new venture. Accepting truth and acknowledging possibilities is just a tiny step forward. Then comes the toughest obstacle: *"Can I do it?"*

Only you are able to answer this question. However, it is really easy to draw a sensible conclusion.

Do a quick comparison. Consider your abilities and record them next to mine of four years ago.

Do you have any authority in your niche? Have you done anything at all which gained you valuable experience? Do you know at least one influential person in this subject area? And have you spoken English since early childhood?

I suppose you answered "yes" at least once. Draw the inevitable conclusion.

Yes, you could be even more socially and professionally inept than I was three years ago. And I tell you: that is actually great news! You don't need godlike qualities to network with other people. You already have everything you need—you are a human. No matter your story, you are capable of connecting with people. We all are, by design. So, if your story is a bit more dramatic than mine, that's good! You will have a more compelling story to tell.

Personally, I could have never told a rag to riches story. I always had food on the table and a roof above my head. I graduated from a decent university. I've always earned more than 150% of the average national salary.

Consequently, it takes effort to make my story sound dramatic. You? You have it easy. Your story *is* compelling.

On the other hand, perhaps you didn't merely answer "yes" to the above questions. If you are an authority, you have experience or some connections, or you finished an English major, then I congratulate you. The question "Can I do it?" simply doesn't apply in your case. Of course you can! If an "average" candidate such as I could do it, your success is almost guaranteed!

Whether you are in a position similar to mine or not, I encourage you to visit my online journal. I started it on April 3, 2013, and have quite diligently kept a record. You can track my journey day by day and judge my skills for yourself. Take notice of my English. I suppose this journal is the only unedited version of my writing on the Net (apart from private social media entries). I know it's quite awful. I remember how red my manuscripts were when they came back from the editor for the first time. Also, keep in mind that the first entry in that journal was written almost eight months after I had begun my journey. My starting point was actually much lower than is recorded there.

Surely you are convinced now: you can do what I did.

I genuinely believe that exceeding my results many times over won't be difficult.

But if you still have doubts, I suggest that these are only in your mind. They are not real. We have already established the facts and they are in your favor. Period. You can't deny that. Nevertheless, you will probably still discuss this with yourself. Maxwell Maltz, the author of *Psycho-Cybernetics*, discovered that people don't act according to the facts but according to how they perceive the facts. More precisely, their beliefs are their facts. How you perceive yourself determines your action. Self-image dictates what you think about yourself and what you do in the outside world. Mr. Maltz was a plastic surgeon. He noticed that some people bettered their lives after improving their look. Others changed nothing about their circumstances and continued to insist they looked horrible. Their false self-image contrasted with reality.

For you? As you can truly change almost any circumstances, any denials come from the false self-image instilled in you by your heritage or social environment. Don't worry, your self-image is fixable.

Networking isn't some top-notch skill like juggling or remembering the content of 300 pages in a matter of minutes. There is no magic to it, no secret formula. Networking is as natural as breathing, talking, or walking. You can do it even if you are handicapped (see: Nick Vujicic). You can do it even if you are crazy busy or a social pansy who cannot approach a stranger even if you only want to offer him a free beer (that would be me).

Networking is an absolutely manageable process that only takes basic human qualities. And you can start wherever you are, which is especially important if you live in the middle of nowhere. I live in Poland. If I want to attend a blogging conference in the USA, I need to get a visa first and pay $2–3k for plane tickets.

My face-to-face skills were nonexistent when I started. I connected with others via the Internet. And 1 forged relationships that allowed me to be featured in a best-selling book and have my books promoted by one of the most successful nonfiction Kindle authors. Networking at live events is much more effective, but it also needs more skills and resources. Comparing live networking with online networking is like comparing brick-and-mortar businesses to online business. You need to invest a lot upfront. And just like a brick-and-mortar business requires a large investment, so does face-to-face networking. Initially, not many of us have such resources or are willing to commit them

Remember:

- Regardless of your skills or training or experience, you can make the contacts you need to make. Others with less ability, resources and experience than you have done so.

Action Items:

- Take a piece of paper.

- Divide it in half and on one side write down a summary of "your starting assets". Even if you're financially struggling, you do have assets. You doubtless have command of English, authority in your niche, experience, knowledge, credentials, social aptitude, etc.

  (On my side of the line, summarize where I began: I had a poor grasp of English; no experience in writing, which was my chosen niche; no knowledge of the publishing game; no credentials; and an introverted 'talks-to-no-one' personality.)

- Compare the two halves. Who seems to have a bigger chance for success?

- If you want an impartial confirmation, put a random name (John or Jane Smith, say) above each list of characteristics.

  Then show the document around and ask for opinions.

  "Which person has the best chance of success?"

3. SHOWING VULNERABILITY IS A KEY TO MAKING CONNECTIONS

Connecting with other people is absurdly easy because we are all similar at the bottom of our hearts. We are vulnerable. High levels of success don't protect you from being hurt. Even rock stars, Hollywood actors, and millionaires are vulnerable. We think that they aren't because they still keep moving forward, but it's not their lack of vulnerability, it's their resilience. We think they have thick skin, and because they are able to bounce back fast from reversals, we don't notice their vulnerability.

This is only normal; they are still humans. No matter how much anyone has achieved, they are not invulnerable. No amount of money or fame will save you from a broken heart or from grief after the death of someone close. Millionaires have problems too. Those problems may not be the ones that occupy an average man—how to pay off debts or save for their children's college education—but they have struggles nonetheless. Having a lot of money creates new problems. The rich may be insecure in their relationships, never knowing for sure if people like them because of their fortune or due to their personal qualities. I listened to a podcast of a millionaire who admitted that, after earning his first million, he had no idea what to do with that amount of money. Do you know that banks in the USA only guarantee deposits up to $250,000? Most people, of course, have no problems with that limit.

Everyone has challenges, and you will never get rid of all your problems. The only people without problems are those in graveyards.

Think about it: without problems, you become complacent. Problems are just signals it's time to move on and grow.

What does vulnerability have to do with networking? Everything. Because everyone has a fear of exposing their authentic self. Anyone who actually does that is perceived as bold. However, he is not doing anything heroic. He is just being himself. If he continues, he will have no regrets at the end of his life. Short and simple: vulnerability is attractive.

I'm a Christian and believe we were created in the image of God, and that God is love. We were created for love, but you cannot love without exposing yourself to loss. Yet life is fairly meaningless if you go through it without giving to others. And doing things for others requires stripping away your layers of protection.

Exposing yourself to loss or hurt is scary. We instinctively avoid that. We are motivated primarily by seeking pleasure and avoiding pain. We are more likely to be interested in signs of danger than in heartwarming stories. Aleks Srbinoski illustrated this very aptly in his book *The 7 Mental Viruses Crushing Your Potential*: "Imagine being in the jungle. You suddenly notice the most beautiful person you have ever seen. Stunning, gorgeous and naked! Then you hear a tiger growl. Where does your attention go?"

This is your big chance. When you demonstrate your vulnerability—when you expose your true self to the world—you become special by default. People admire you. People respect you. People are attracted to you. It's because *everybody* wishes deep in their souls to be like you. You won't find any exceptions.

You see, everybody has this deep desire to live an authentic life, but very few do. There are a multitude of reasons for that, but they all come down to different ways of avoiding pain. The human brain's default option is avoiding pain (remember the tiger?), so the majority goes along this path (and regrets it on their deathbed).

You can probably see how the economic law of supply and demand could work to your advantage. A few authentic folk will be in demand, appealing to the masses who don't lead true lives. When you are authentic and vulnerable you have the precious "commodity" everybody desires. You become valuable, just because you are yourself! People *will* want to connect with you, they *will* want to do business with you, they *will* want to buy *your* stuff.

The automatic reaction to this train of thought is, "But, am I not manipulating and abusing those who read the words I write?" Of course not, silly! That's why it is called authenticity ("real or genuine; not copied or false; true and accurate"—according to Meriam-Webster's dictionary).

You are not able to manipulate or abuse when you are genuine.

To do so, you would have to first inform your interlocutor that you have such intent. You cannot manipulate anyone who knows your plans in advance. But this is an extreme and highly hypothetical example. As I stated above, I believe you were designed for love. Be honest with others, be honest with yourself, and express your true motives. You will be on the safe side each time..

Remember:

- We are all vulnerable, and, when revealed, this is attractive to others because no one fears those who open their defenses.

Action Items:

- Think again about the things that matter.
- Consider what supporting these values has cost you—or could cost you if you openly defended them or devoted more time to them. Now consider how you'll talk about why this cost is worth paying.

4. EFFECTIVENESS STEMS FROM BEING AUTHENTIC

I'm fond of Stephen R. Covey's core message that integrity is the foundation of trust. Mr. Covey dedicated the first three parts of *The 7 Habits of Highly Effective People* not to the time management gimmicks so often mandated for effectiveness, but to the methods of living one's life with integrity. How does integrity make anyone effective? Simply put: people trust individuals with integrity. Trust eliminates the friction from the cooperation process.

Imagine this situation: everyone in your team at the office is your good friend. Is cooperation easy? Does your work get done fast?

What is true in a small team of several people is also true in enterprises and corporations. At the end of every business process are people, whose effectiveness increases the more they trust each other. Trust is the lifeblood of effectiveness. Integrity breeds trust.

If you don't trust (pun intended) Mr. Covey, take a look at some of the great people of the last century: Blessed Teresa of Calcutta, Mahatma Gandhi, Nelson Mandela, Jim Rohn, Martin Luther King. They didn't just preach, they lived what they were preaching. They are textbook examples of integrity. Were their works effective? Bah, they were even prodigious. Examine their stories. What resources did they have at the beginning? Next to none, in most cases, but they were able to change the ways of whole nations.

If you want to network effectively, you need to live with integrity.

This is quite important in the age of digital communication. The anonymity of the Internet is a constant temptation. You may get the idea that creating an alter ego that is more handsome, cleverer, or more impressive is more profitable. And it is very easy to create a virtual personality. It seems like a perfect shortcut to great results: instead of growing into a man or woman of value, all you need to do is to pretend that you already are. You can buy anonymous domain names and create fake social media accounts. You can even create multiple email addresses under the same domain and pretend that your one-man show is a promising start-up which has hired a dozen people.

You can fake it all very easily, but you can be easily verified as well. And it takes just one breech in your "virtual" wall to blow away your credibility. That's why James Altucher calls social media "individual media"; media is no longer possessed by faceless entities. Each social media account has a face assigned to it. But this face needs a full human behind it to entice trust and to work effectively.

Jeff Goins, in his book *You Are a Writer*, said that in the end *you* are your brand. Either you stand behind what you say and your deeds are compatible with your words, or your brand is in shambles, unlikely to produce any meaningful results.

Authenticity goes beyond pursuing results.

Eliminating friction from your interactions brings other advantages. The main one is that you free up your brain's capacity when you act with integrity 24/7. When all you want is to genuinely reach out and provide value to others, and when you treat each partner in your network like a real person, you save up a lot of brainpower. When you don't need to plot and scheme, to lie or pretend, you can focus on providing value. This is your competitive advantage. Everyone on this planet has just 24 hours each day. Scheming and lying consumes time and energy. If your competitors choose that path, they are automatically putting themselves at a disadvantage. They have less time for the actions that really drive their businesses forward.

I am no authority on business ethics or business models. However, the emphasis on authenticity is not just my empty and uninformed opinion. I'm adding my voice to the growing trend towards authenticity.

One of its forerunners is Kim Grast, the author of *Will the Real You Stand Up?* Kim is a media consultant and an expert in social media. She advises entrepreneurs and small businesses on how to effectively brand themselves in the world of modern media. She does it for a living. The core message of her book is that authenticity and integrity are key, regardless of the size of the marketing budget. She points out many instances when big corporations failed at this—even with vast resources—yet tiny companies grew rapidly by being consistently on message.

Kim Grast is not a lone idealist. James Altucher and Jeff Goins, whom I mentioned above, are riding the same trend. Susan RoAne, the networking specialist, preached the same message even prior to the Internet age. My friend Matt Stone, who has launched a few profitable online businesses in the last few years, is also a big proponent of this approach. Practically his whole book *Internet Business Shortcut* is a brochure that advertises genuine networking and value production as a way to thrive in an online environment.

Remember:

- Integrity is the foundation of trust. It is your competitive advantage.
- People trust individuals with integrity. You may not have anything to share that is new, yet everyone who talks about life and values and purpose brings a unique voice. The factor that makes your message different from all other messages is "you".
- At the end of every business process are people and trust is the lifeblood of effectiveness.
- A fake Internet personality may be easy to create, but it is just as easy to expose.

Action Items:

- Consider the message you want to share. Why will people have a reason to listen? NOTE: The more of "yourself" you get into your message, the more attractive it becomes.

5. THERE ARE PLENTY OF PEOPLE YOU'LL CLICK WITH

Another advantage of authenticity at work is that you don't have to care about the authenticity of your partners. It's not that you act like a naive Polyanna. But when you act with integrity, sensing the other side's dishonesty is easy. All you need to do in that case is compare their words and deeds. When they disappoint, don't blacklist them. Give them a second chance. If you are a good Christian, you can even give them 77 chances. But you will never be fooled by them. Your own integrity acts as a perfect BS detector.

However, birds of a feather flock together. Duplicitous people can't stand honesty. I was contacted on Facebook a few weeks ago by a woman who noticed my entries on Jim Rohn's Facebook page. She told me an inspiring story about how she saw Jim live a few times and how her husband worked with him for several years. She also suggested I follow her new mentor who was supposedly Jim-like. Well, I checked the guy and my BS detector tingled very loudly. His free mentorship program sounded like an online Ponzi scheme to me. It was totally unlike Jim Rohn. A couple of weeks later, I got back to her, and told her as nicely as I could that I'm not interested. What is more, I described my feelings towards the supposed mentor. She never replied.

You don't need to worry about contacting unauthentic people. But what about those who are authentic, but, how to say it politely… jerks? You don't need to do business with them. There are over seven billion people on our planet. You will find some (a few hundred thousand) nice ones. Do you recall the lesson about the right use of your time as a competitive advantage? Don't waste your time on braggarts, no matter how rich and influential they are.

When I was making my first steps into the online marketing world, I got on the list of a millionaire. His pitching emails were full of concern about me: "I sell so hard, because I know I have the greatest opportunity for you, and I feel you will be disadvantaged if you don't try this, blah, blah, blah."

On his contact page there was "reassuring" information that his team replies to each email in 24 to 48 hours. I wanted to know more;

I sent them an email. They never responded. After his big product launch, he sent me an email with the worst pitch I have ever read in my life. Between the lines he basically said that I was a poor loser because I hadn't bought his high-end product, but there was one last chance for me: I should buy an access to the behind-the-scenes material he shares with his high-profile clients, so maybe I could unlearn being a sucker. Only $299 a month! Yikes!

Don't get me wrong. Based on the available data, I think he may provide decent value to his clients. They actually get results. But if the price of success is to become someone like him… Thanks, but no thanks.

Not wasting time with the wrong people applies to all interactions. The role of an initial contact is not to become best buddies, but to feel if the chemistry between you is right. If it's not, don't try to force it. Get over your incompatibility and go looking for people with whom you connect with little effort. There are seven billion people, remember? The sooner you discover that the guy or gal on the other side doesn't share your point of view and values, the better. You will waste less time on building a relationship that is doomed to fail anyway. You don't send someone a survey about their values. You interact with them to determine if they are the right candidate for a long-term friendship. Don't be afraid to call it that. In the end what are the longest and best relationships? Friendships. You are on a quest to build them.

When approaching new people for the first time, be authentic. Of course, don't tell them your life story in the first meeting, but beware of duplicity (I mean, on your part). Do not hold yourself back, especially in regard to the issues you consider important. Do not think about being liked. If you hide yourself behind a social mask, only two things can happen and neither is beneficial:

1. You will pretend to be someone else for so long that you will become someone else, a person who drifted away from your original values and beliefs.

2. One day you will take off the mask and demonstrate your true self. The relationship you have been trying to cultivate will be endangered and probably will end badly, because the other person thought you were someone different.

On the other hand, when being authentic, both of you will be able to "assess" the chemistry between you. Both of you will judge sensibly if keeping the relationship alive is the right decision.

Very often, there is a valid concern: "Can this person stand such a raw honesty on my part?" We are so used to political correctness and empty diplomatic gestures, that being authentic, transparent, raw, and honest seems like an aberration. And maybe it is. Use your own judgment in each interaction. I prefer the direct approach. When I see an issue, I name it. I don't beat around the bush. That's the most direct route and the fastest one. I'm not afraid of turning somebody off. If I speak the truth about myself and our relationship and they can't stand that, they are not the right partner for me.

One day I pitched a guest post idea to a guy I followed. It was about my reflection on the nightmare the legal system often became for small businesses. He replied "I don't want to advise people against using lawyers even though that's what I believe myself."

Inside, an alarm went off in my head.

The man believed what I was saying, but didn't want to convey the same advice to his audience?! I respected him and I was concerned about him. This was dual thinking which usually ends up badly. Out of my concern, I answered quite bluntly:

"I'm concerned about what you've said. It seems like your brand is not congruent with your personal beliefs. If I were you, I would modify either your brand or beliefs. It's very unhealthy for mental health to be of two minds about something."

Not very diplomatic, was it? But that's who I am. Diplomacy is not my strength. Luckily, the blogger didn't get offended. We still kept in touch and several months later I landed a different guest post on his site. Our mutual respect only increased.

That's what happens when you act in accordance with your deepest beliefs and values. I could have lost this relationship by giving my unsolicited and harsh advice. I remember being hesitant about sending my reply: "What will he think of me? What if he is offended?"

But I couldn't just pretend that everything was alright. I was genuinely concerned about him. What if he didn't realize his own ambiguity? Down the road, his stance could have caused him real troubles, both in business and his personal life. I did what I felt was best for both of us.

Try to always be 100% authentic. Honesty will spare you a lot of potential misunderstandings. Remember the first regret of the dying: "I wish I'd had the courage to live a life true to myself, not the life others expected of me."

Be yourself. This benefits you and others.

This is a book about building business connections. And of course you can do business without authenticity. Look around. Ninety-five percent of businesses are doing just that. I've used the services of about a dozen financial institutions so far. Their ads were full of goodwill. Their declarations were reassuring. But when they had an opportunity to suck money out of my wallet, they did it in a heartbeat (and they pretended they were sorry about that).

In the United States, 70% of employees are not satisfied with the job they are doing. And dissatisfied employees don't engage in their work. Well, the USA is a happy country, as everywhere else this percentage is even higher. I've worked in several big companies and had dealings with a dozen more. I can count on the fingers of one hand people who were authentic at their workplace. Everybody pretends. Everybody plays games. Everybody wants to take the advantage. That's the standard.

It's also ineffective.

This is not a book for CEOs of Fortune 500 companies. I assume you are a small business owner, a solopreneur or even just a wannapreneur. At the beginning of your journey, you will be interacting with other bloggers, podcasters, and authors. Even if you start to interact with bigger entities, you will be in contact with their low-level staff. When you want to put your article on Huffington Post, you are not facing the board of directors, but an editor. The best course of action is connecting on the human level. Be authentic and let them judge if they want to work with you. Business interactions are another step up. But if you have human relationships figured out, it's easier to forge a working relationship.

Yes, it can sometimes work in the opposite direction—do the business first and then forge the friendship—but that's a way with fewer successes. If you haven't figured out how you feel about yourself upfront, the risk of friction in a business relationship is exponentially higher.

Remember:

- • People reveal themselves through their deeds, not their words. Watch what people do.
- • Don't waste your time on those who posture, no matter how rich and influential they are.
- • Think of your initial contact with someone as the chance to mingle, so you can feel if the chemistry between you is all right.
- • Be yourself. This will inevitably serve you and others best.

Action Items:

- • Who do you want to connect with?
- • You might need to learn something, or sell something, or find assistance for a task you have ahead. What will you bring to the relationship, and how can you demonstrate this ahead of time?

6. THE GREATEST GIFT YOU HAVE IS YOURSELF

When I was starting my transformation, very little could be said in my favor. What kind of life experience did I have? I'm a white male who graduated from university with a degree in IT. My only "struggle" was that I started my family early and our parents couldn't support us financially very much. The only praiseworthy long-term activity I was involved in was attending the same church community for over fifteen years. My personal philosophy at that time was "Just get by another day." I was intelligent, but I didn't use my intelligence very much. I tried to avoid thinking at all, while indulging myself with computer games and TV shows. I didn't have the skills I needed to exist in the modern online world. I had no social media account. I'd never heard of WordPress. I hadn't written a single blog post or recorded a single audio or video. My English was self-taught with some help from my teachers (I began learning English from the beginning three times, in each school level I attended). I had no achievements worth mentioning. In my IT career of eight years, I had attended only a few courses and never contemplated taking any exams. I was overweight, led a sedentary lifestyle, and loved sweets (I still love them, but now it's a platonic love). As you can tell from this brief analysis, my mindset and character weren't top notch.

How much value could such a fellow provide? Well, to tell the truth, not much. At the beginning I wasn't a fountain of value for others. I could only serve as an object lesson: "Don't do as this guy did." It took about four months from the time I decided I needed to pull myself together until I published my first blog post (which wasn't very valuable, by the way). I spent those months on my personal development.

Does this mean that if you spent the last several years living according to the "get by" philosophy, you are sentenced to a four-month-long intensive personal development program?

Nope. You are valuable. You are precious. We all are. You just need to come to terms with this idea: your personal experience, whatever it was until today, is your treasure. You don't need to present knowledge in order to provide value to others. Knowledge is freely available everywhere. You just have to be yourself and be vulnerable. When someone preaches to me, "We should carefully consider all the dependencies in the family dynamics when discovering that a family member is gay," it is meaningless nonsense.

However, when my friend told me that her brother is gay and it's hard on her, her personal experience immediately made it more relevant for me.

If I had chosen to be open and share about the subjects where I was ahead of the majority—like early parenting, getting a higher education, or trusting that God was leading my life in the right direction—I could have provided value to others right away. Those four months of personal development were less about me becoming valuable and more about giving myself permission to share my experience with others.

How does one provide value? What if you have nothing to say? In my view, you are never without the potential to add to the conversation. If you don't have new facts or knowledge to bring, you can always bring gratitude, appreciation, encouragement, and a positive attitude. This world is a desert when it comes to such qualities. We can never have too much of these things.

You can read what others write about themselves. Even the most successful authors, actors, and artists confess that they still don't feel secure about their art. They remain—despite their successes—easily hurt by criticism, and are always positively influenced by the warm feedback from their fans.

Nevertheless, your "positivity boost" must be genuine to truly bring value to others. It must come from your heart, not just from your mouth. It can really go a long way. My writing career started because my friend told me my articles were interesting and encouraged me to expand them into a book. I needed that gentle, positive prodding to take action. My friend's one sentence led to more than 15,000 readers. This is the value you wield when you encourage another individual. Alone with my thoughts, I was prone to discouragement and likely to talk myself out of any serious attempts. You are valuable; your honest encouragement is valuable.

Should you spill your experiences in front of everybody as soon as possible? Well, it works for some. I have a friend who has a hard time shutting up. He talks incessantly and he has been acting that way for years. Judging by their video content, a lot of industry leaders also have plenty to say. I'm biased—I strongly dislike wordiness. I like to be direct and concise. But I'm an introvert male. My tendency is to limit interactions to a few gestures and grunts. I advise that you assess your tendencies and act accordingly.

I avoid fluff. Beating around the bush wastes both your time and the time of those who consume your content or speak with you. Empty chatter does not equal value. Take, for example, Amazon customer reviews. Many times they are cluttered by personal ruminations that have nothing to do with the book. You scroll down and down looking for the insight, which seems to be lost in the multitude of words. Quantity rarely transforms magically into quality. Avoid writing hype. The most worthless reviews are those with the most exclamation marks: "I read it!!! It was great!!! It changed my life!!!" Heck, but how and why?!!

The value-providing rule I practice is "Say nothing, if you have nothing to say."

"You can never get too much editing and feedback."—Guy Kawasaki, author, marketing specialist

Another piece of value that everyone can offer, even if they are just starting or have no clue about the point of discussion, is feedback. Your unique perspective is always valuable. You may not have experience or skills, but you always have an opinion. Make sure you provide it in a respectful and useful way. "Because I say so" is rarely of much value.

You don't need any fancy equations or elaborate infographics. Just say what you think. Every adult can provide value to others by doing this. You just donate your time to express your feedback. The most valuable form of feedback is the report you give after implementing someone's advice. You not only validate the original idea that way, you add to it, as each case study adds some unique personal insight to the existing content. Doing something, getting some results, and sharing this fact is a fireproof method of providing value.

Remember:

- • Your personal experience, whatever it has been, is your treasure.
- • You always have potential to add to the conversation.
- • You can always bring gratitude, appreciation, encouragement and a positive attitude.
- • Donate your time to express your feedback as positive feedback is greatly valued.

Action Items:

- Identify some individuals who have told a story you like or shared a principle you support. Perhaps they are bloggers, Facebook 'friends', or forum participants.

7. THINK FIRST THIS: HOW CAN YOU SERVE?

I have just one rule of thumb when it comes to adding value to influencers who are ahead of you in terms of success: don't drive your own agenda.

Whenever you try to push your own points, your contributions risk being taken as fluff, hype, and irrelevance. And those "above you" in the pecking order are usually quite busy, so pitching your feeble idea is just another annoying nuisance consuming their time. It doesn't work. How do I know? Ahh, well, I'm guilty. The only benefit I got out of my clunky attempts to drive my agenda was that I was able to target the nicest people in the world worth following. Everyone who answers your pitch is worth staying in touch with. The nicest people were even apologetic about declining my stupid offers.

In a perfect world, each of your attempts to reach out will come from the goodness of your heart and be without a pinch of self-interest. You may not be able to provide value with every interaction, but your success ratio will be much higher than if you let your ego intrude all the time.

Needless to say, we don't live in a perfect world. You need to smuggle your stuff onto the agenda somehow. Acting without requiring a result for yourself is more satisfying, but it's a risky proposition if you want to make some money.

In our imperfect world, you can admit you have needs. Your partners have them too. The success of networking comes from reconciling your needs. But to avoid being considered a dolt, try to put the interest of your partners first. Aim for a win-win situation.

The easiest way to provide value is to know their needs in advance and answer to them. You do that by keeping in touch with them. Follow your digital mentor according to their content schedule (a blog post twice a week or a podcast episode every week) and you will know what they want. I've done that countless times and it always worked like a charm.

Just follow this simple formula:

1. Find ways to interact with them that you feel comfortable with.

If they are active on LinkedIn and you don't yet have an account, this might not be the best place for you to connect. Even if you create an account, you will be clumsy in an unfamiliar environment. Personally, I love to connect via blog comments. I can access blogs anytime from anywhere. I love to communicate in writing. I'm a freak who loves to read and learn, so I actually feel like I'm rewarding myself each time I read an interesting blog post. Blog comments are for me an ideal and effortless way to connect with others. Supposedly, only about 1% of visitors bother to leave a blog comment, so by this simple activity I am able to appear on the radar of some "big" folks.

2. Show up.

If you just do this, you will be ahead of the pack. When I decide to connect with someone, I don't just leave a single blog comment and send an email the next day. I comment on each new post for a few weeks. I often search the archive for interesting articles and comment on them. When I finally send an email, the blogger definitely knows who I am.

3. Build a habit.

This is the tool that will allow you to show up regularly. I won't get deep into the details of building a habit, as all you need to know will be included in the fifth part of the *Six Simple Steps to Success* series. Just be mindful of the basic elements of habit development: create a trigger, define your routine, design a reward, and track your performance.

For my commenting habit, I use the Coach.me app for all of the above. My trigger is going through my habit list in the application. When I see I haven't commented yet, it ignites me to find and read an appropriate blog post. After commenting I mark the habit off on the Coach.me list and the sense of accomplishment connected with this activity is my reward. Coach.me also serves as a tracking tool.

The most precious gift you can give to someone is your time and attention. If you combine both factors, your input is valuable no matter what. By consciously cultivating relationships on a regular basis, you are laying the groundwork. It's much easier to provide value when there is a bond of trust between you than if you have to overcome the friction of unfamiliarity and wariness. In this process of cultivating the relationship, you will discover what your potential partner needs. You will be surprised how often you'll be able to lend a hand. Share their stuff. Sign up to their email list, and actually read their emails. (Hint: if you can't stand their correspondence, this is a sign you are not a good match.) Reply to them. Answer their pleas for feedback. Take their surveys. Give an opinion about their products or services. Purchase their offers if you need them and will use them.

I advise you not to initiate contact if there is no win in the interaction for the other side. If you can't answer the question, "What's in it for them?" don't even bother with opening your email client. Nevertheless, if you follow anybody long enough, I bet you will know their "wants" just like that, without too much thought.

When I want something from the people I follow, it is usually the benefit of their audience. Most entrepreneurs will take you up on this if you offer something their followers can use. You will have a deal secured almost before you ask. If they agree, you will know you are working with someone who is service-oriented rather than focused on their own self-interest.

By going all-out for the benefit of others, you won't come across as sleazy. When you approach someone with their genuine interest in mind, it's detectable. I can't tell you exactly how this "BS detector" works, but when you are genuine, it just doesn't tingle.

Remember:

- • Don't drive your agenda.
- • Use the same media.
- • Show up consistently.
- • The most precious gift you could have ever give to someone is your time and attention.

Action Items:

- • Make a detailed plan for following one of the people you've found common ground with:
- Where you will follow them, and what will you aim to contribute?
- How often will you stay in touch?
- How will you keep track of your following efforts?

8. STAY ON THE RADAR AND YOU'LL INEVITABLY BE SEEN

"You are the average of the five people you spend the most time with."— Jim Rohn

I have found the above crumb of Jim's wisdom to be true. It reveals the real core of networking: you are in it for the people you meet, not for the bargains you might get. Interactions mold and change you; they determine who you are. Choose the members of your network carefully and mindfully. If you hang around cool people, you will become cooler.

I urge you to stay on the radar of the people you consider important. You should keep in touch with them continually— forever—and plan your networking habits accordingly. The only excuse for letting the relationship lapse is that they (or you) change enough that they are no longer the right partner for you. When Anakin Skywalker became Darth Vader, Princess Padmé and Obi Wan Kenobi didn't stay around.

If you outgrow your peers, you'll naturally spend less time on them. When I was living just to get by, my favorite pastime was a card game. Every weekend I could spare, I met with my buddies and played cards. But when I got busy with writing my books, I reduced my get-togethers to just a few times a year.

Estimating the outcomes of social relationships is hard. One day I found a very tender comment about the human condition on my buddy's blog that had been left by a woman named Naomi. I checked out her site, and it was about starting a business, nothing I was immediately interested in. Her comment however convinced me that she was an extraordinary human being. I signed up to her RSS feed and began visiting her blog regularly. One day, I found an interesting post on her site about integrating your blog's archive with Buffer, so you could tweet your old content no matter how long ago it was published. It took me a couple hours of tinkering, but I implemented this solution. A few weeks later my blog post was retweeted by a rock star with a couple of million followers. To this day, I'm not sure if my site crashed because of the surge of traffic, or due to the sloppiness of my provider.

Appearing on someone's radar is really as simple as sharing their stuff, doing them small favors, and answering their calls to action. I noticed that a blogger will often leave a question at the end of a post. The blogger is trying to start a conversation with his readers. I also noticed that 80% of commenters ignore such questions. People are so eager to say their thing that they ignore what the other side wants to know. Here's my tip: be in the 20% of those who answer on topic and you will inevitably appear on the radar.

If you target the right people, there will be no shame in sharing their stuff. And if you feel uneasy about sharing their stuff—for instance, you think it's too bold or too controversial—then that's a signal you are not a good fit for them. Sharing is caring, as the saying goes. It's true. Every blogger and every online entrepreneur worth their salt will notice someone consistently sharing their stuff. And bam! You are on the radar.

Just be wary of showing off. You must be genuine, authentic. You must find their stuff interesting. You must be willing to interest others with the information you are sharing. Show your investment by adding some personal comment to your share. Recommend it to your followers and acquaintances. You can skip that part, but the difference in impact will be visible. You will be a smaller dot on their radar screen.

Where could you share their stuff?

1. Where you are.

Why register on LinkedIn to share someone's stuff when you have other, more feasible options? Because of my limited schedule, I have just a few social and para-social (like Livefyre or Disquis commenting networks) media accounts. I very often share on Twitter; it's my default option. I only sporadically share stuff on Facebook, because I'm less often there. I very rarely visit my G+ profile, so I don't often share there.

2. Where you can.

If among the sharing buttons there are no platforms you

habitually use, choose the one platform the owner prefers. When I comment on TrafficGenerationCafe I use Google+ because it's the only option available there. Sometimes I find an interesting blog that I could follow, but the only option is through a channel I can't or don't want to use. For example, some platforms use Facebook commenting system. I keep a low profile on Facebook, so I don't comment on such platforms.

3. Where you have some impact.

Going back to my LinkedIn example, what's the use of registering there when you have no presence? You don't add value this way. Your share will go into the void. No one else will see the stuff you've shared because no one else is connected to you at that platform. Choose the medium, where your opinion and audience have some weight.

4. Where you'll benefit.

It's not by accident that this is the last point on the list. First and foremost, keep in mind the interest of your audience and of the people whose content you share. Once you've done that, you have the freedom to choose among the options more or less advantageous for you. I love to comment on sites that provide a backlink to my site. If I have a few options to choose from, I always use the one that leaves the track back to my site.

For example on my friend's site, StartBizQuitJob.com, providing a link to your site is obligatory when you comment.

Naomi Dinsmore April 13, 2014 at 10:35 pm #   REPLY ↰

Hi Michal,

So glad this helps. BufferApp is great and they have fantastic customer support too. If you have any trouble installing, let me know and I'll help you.

Naomi

Naomi Dinsmore recently posted...1 Smart way for Keeping Old Content New Using This WordPress Plugin ⊚

Michal   REPLY ↰
Twitter: StawickiMichal
April 27, 2014 at 2:23 pm #

Naomi, I did everything as you explained, but it doesn't work. Is there an easy way to test the configuration?
I mean, other than waiting 4 hours if something really landed on my Twitter?

Michal recently posted...My 4 Pillars to Staying Consistent ⊚

She also uses CommentLuv for her comments system, so when I leave a comment on her site the plugin searches the latest posts on my site and provides a link to the specific post (I can choose from among the last ten).

Next in the order of influence is your feedback. It's never worthless. Even if dozens of people in a blogger's (or podcaster's) audience say the same thing, your voice is not lost. The bigger the audience, the more data points are needed. When it comes to choosing one option among three, it matters if a dozen or fifteen people voted for a particular option. I tell you that from my own experience. My dear subscribers helped me to choose the title for my book about developing consistency traits (the winning title was *The Art of Persistence*). When just 50 or 60 people vote for 3 or 4 options, every voice helps in making the right decision.

You don't need to wait for permission to give your feedback. On the contrary—the most valuable feedback is the one you've given without being prompted. Your feedback might also be something the other person didn't have a clue about, or an angle they hadn't considered. I connected with an author who quit his corporate job to pursue "his thing." He planned to earn $100,000 in the first year. He did that in half that time. I pointed out that it seemed like an overnight success story and maybe in his next post he should paint a broad picture about how long it really took him to amass his experience and learn his skills. He answered me: "Great idea, I never really thought about the time it took to become a strong speaker, or to amass my experience. Kind of hard to quantify, but definitely worth mentioning because I'm a much better speaker now than I was two years ago, and there were specific people I gave thousands of dollars to who made me better."

The next level is giving encouragement. People always need validation of their ideas. They always love to get some support, even if it's just verbal. Bloggers who've just started building their audience, authors whose job is lonely by its nature, entrepreneurs nervous about their latest business idea; we all need outside confirmation that we're doing a good job, that our work is indeed helpful, useful, or uplifting. I've sold thousands of books but have received only hundreds of positive reviews. And I've had just a few dozen personal encouraging messages. Encouragement is much rarer and more precious than money.

Alright, it's time for the ultimate way to appear on someone's radar. Do this one thing, and you not only will get noticed, but you will be bumped straight to the inner circle. You won't be like a point on their radar; you will be like a supernova. This is one thing which no influencer, no matter how busy or big he is, can ignore. The magic trick is implementation.

I got a personal letter from David Allen, the author of *Getting Things Done*, after I sent him an email saying that his book had made a difference in my life (because it had) and that I had written an ultra-short book about time management tips. I thought this part might catch his attention: "In the past year, I have written over 150,000 words, maintained three blogs, and written five eBooks, despite all the other things vying for my time. Additionally, I have gotten back in shape and reconnected more meaningfully than ever with my family and spirituality."

My friend, Kurt Frankenberg, pulled the same "trick" with Ana , an expert on Search Engine Optimization. He read her ultra-detailed blogs full of actionable tips and implemented them one by one on his website. His traffic almost doubled within a short time. Then he dropped her a message. Voilà, he not only appeared on her radar, he was invited to do a guest post on her site which attracts about half a million visitors a month.

Of course, in order to make this tactic effective you have to do the homework. I really had written 150,000 words and 5 eBooks before contacting David. Kurt really did double the traffic to his site. The whole reason this method is so effective is because everybody has goodwill, but only a very few have the balls to go out and do something. Whenever you present yourself as a doer, you shine among the throng of talkers.

Remember:

- • You are in it for the people you meet, not for the bargains you might get.
- • Appearing on someone's radar is as simple as answering their calls to take action.
- • Share, give feedback and implement what influencers teach.

Action Items:

- • Design a game plan for staying on the radar. For each influencer you want to follow write down these things:
- The place you will share their stuff
- Your method for giving feedback and encouragement
- Your plan for doing the above regularly
- The steps you can take NOW to start your plan.

9. TRUE FRIENDSHIP CAN ONLY HAPPEN IF YOU'RE GENUINE

I don't know about you, but for me the word *relationship* is synonymous with friendship. My favorite definition of *friend* is, "Someone who knows everything about you and still likes you." When it comes to initiating the real contact after you've appeared on your friend's radar, it must be natural. You can't wait for your would-be partner to ask if you have some agenda. What kind of friend is someone who must be asked every time if he needs help or has something to say or contribute? In a relationship that is working well, you don't need to ask for permission, you just articulate your proposition or need, and discuss it. Don't think too much; don't weigh the correctness of each step. And in this I include initiation of the project. If you have something valuable to bring to the table, go ahead. If you think it will not be a burden for your partner, ask for a favor or for help.

Of course, when we talk about online relationships, the bonds are much harder to establish, and much weaker at the beginning. You are not friends because you commented on someone's posts or tweeted about them. You can't go to them and ask to borrow a huge sum of money. Just act friendly. Be sensible about it. Friendship means you care enough not to ask for something which could strain or hurt them.

On the other hand, don't be timid. Show your real self, like I did with the blogger who rejected my guest post. *Vulnerability and authenticity are the bridges to friendship.* It's hard to build a relationship without some level of openness. Be yourself. I have a weird sense of humor and I like to send "my" kind of joke in the second or third email. If they get me, we will build rapport faster. If they don't, I can consider backing off the relationship at an early stage. My humor is *that* weird. I know (from sad experience) that people can't always sense when I'm serious and when I'm not, and they can be offended. This testing the waters prevents hurt feelings and wasted time.

At the beginning you are not friends, but you should act with a friendship mindset. Be vulnerable. Be helpful. Be caring. We all have

BS detectors, and they are always on, even through digital communication. Emanate authenticity, and the other person will sense this. Don't be afraid of being hurt. In fact, it's a good thing. "What doesn't kill you ..." and so on. I love it when people hurt my feelings at the very beginning of our relationship. It can only mean one of two things:

1. I'm doing something wrong (have too high expectations?) and can improve upon their feedback.

2. They are wrong people (for me) to connect with, which is good to learn.

Both options are a win.

If you have some business in mind or a favor to ask, it's natural you initiate the contact. You must reach out first, which raises a dilemma. First of all, do you have the right to ask? Is it a reasonable request or is it the kind of request comparable to begging Anthony Robbins for a million dollars (or even a thousand), because you are his fan?

Once again, use a friendship measurement. Would you ask your friend for such a thing? It is one thing to ask for a review of your book and another to request that they share your book with their audience of 20,000. You have different levels of relationships and the request should be appropriate to the level. We are social animals and we instinctively feel how much trust we've built with someone, who is creditor and who is debtor in the relationship. Trust your guts.

The same goes when they contact you. Estimate the emotional bank balance between you. Consider if their request is justified. You'll know when your partner is overboard with their demands. On the other hand, you'll also know when the favor is so small that it is not even worth mentioning. Act accordingly.

If you're like most others, you're full of self-doubt. It may hinder your networking attempts significantly. Most of the time, this doubt is just a mind trick put up by your lazy subconscious. If it can discourage you from actions such as writing an email, it will save a ton of energy. It's so much easier to tell yourself, "Who am I to ask for that?" "What would they think about me?" or "I don't deserve this" than it is to sit down, write the email, and send it to the recipient.

And so, I will reiterate: just be vulnerable; that's the best strategy. When you allow yourself to be judged by others, when you are honest about your fears, you disarm your subconscious. I remember when I reached out to bloggers about my book launch for the first time (January 2013). At that time I was selling fewer than a couple hundred copies of my books and my self-esteem was anything but invincible. I added a PS to my plea:

"I feel out of my comfort zone asking you for help. This is an indicator that it was a wise move on my part :D "

And I tell you, that worked very well. I had 100% success—all three bloggers agreed to help me to some extent. That book became my first bestseller.

Another helpful hack: Imagine the negative feedback you fear. I've done my fair share of pitching and cold pitching to bloggers, authors, and influencers. The worst thing I've met with is gentle criticism from a couple of guys I deeply respect, which was painful. They told me right to my face that I wasn't in a position to ask them for such big favors. Their disapproval was an opportunity for me to repent and deepen our relationships. The people who didn't know me? They simply ignored me. Indifference wasn't painful at all. You'll find that 99% of the time the most likely result is indifference; that's not much to worry about.

If diminishing the feared negatives doesn't work, try emphasizing the potential positives. To motivate yourself to action, ponder how your message could add value for your partner, or even better, for his/ her audience. Then remind yourself that if you neglect to reach out, they will be left without this value.

Remember:

- Vulnerability and authenticity are the bridges to friendship
- Trust your gut feelings.
- Asking for a favor often requires you to overcome self-doubts.

Action Items:

- Make a list of three people you would like to connect with.
- For each, note why the connection will be beneficial to them.
- Plan how you're going to make the contact, and make it!

10. BEFORE YOU TRY TO SELL, SHARE THE THINGS THAT SERVE

The most important element in reaching out is avoiding being pushy. Don't ever go with just a "buy, buy, buy" message. I'm not just talking about a selling proposition in the literal sense. Every time you communicate only your agenda, you are being pushy and will be perceived as a sleazy salesman. If you can't see a win in the deal for your partner, you'd better refrain from sending the message altogether.

Don't start without a clear message that describes their potential win. The only way to go forward without this, that I see, would be an open admission that you can't see a win for them, but that you're hoping they will be nice and comply with your request. In return, you promise to compensate them for this favor in the future. But it doesn't sound like a perfect pitch, does it? This is probably only a useful method for desperate times. For every other time, find their win in the deal and emphasize it.

How do you come up with a "win" to offer? Put yourself in their shoes. Spend just a couple of minutes reflecting about how you would react to the message you're about to send. For example, imagine yourself as Pat Flynn of the Smart Passive Income blog sitting in his office. You (as Pat Flynn) have a business generating over a million dollars in revenue, you manage a team of five to ten people, you have an audience numbering hundreds of thousands, and you receive this message:

"Hi, Pat,

I appreciate the great job you do and how you so generously share your knowledge.

I'm an author and I've just written my first children's book. It's titled *Pink Unicorn* and it's going live next week. I know you have small children, so I thought you would be interested in reading and reviewing it.

Best Regards,

Your Fanboy"

Well, imagine that. I would just delete such an email, but I'm a jerk. I suppose there's a remote chance that Pat will be in a "family mood" and decide to read the book to his daughter. But appealing to the needs of his audience would have a much better chance of success. Having some substance in your support, like being a successful author of children's books who, thanks to Pat's advice, built an impressive online presence and now is reaping the benefits, seems even more compelling. If you could also summarize how you built this presence and offer it to Pat's audience in an easy to digest way, like an infographic, your chances further increase.

So, draft your message first, and then read it from the perspective of the receiver and ponder if you would comply with such a request. Would you have been interested? Would you have been willing to take action based on it? Would you have found value for your audience in it? If the answers are affirmative, push the send button. If not, rethink your offer or the way you present it.

Make sure you personalize your messages too. The "smaller" you are, the more personalized your messages should be. If you've been taking massive action, are recognized in your niche as an authority, and are ready to reach out to 100 influencers, you might not have the time to produce 100 personalized messages. But if you are a beginner, you might only reach out to 10 people because you don't know anyone else. This level of activity is more manageable. Just keep balance between your resources (especially time) and the size of your campaign. When I reached out for the first time to three bloggers, I wrote a script, pasted it into my email client, and changed about half of the message to reflect our relationship in detail. When I asked my email subscribers to volunteer for beta reading of my book for the first time, I sent a broadcast first, and then I answered each email personally. I had a core of my reply ready—"I need you to do this and that, please pay attention to this issue"—but I personalized each one.

My email list has grown 400% since that time. Now I send a broadcast and if the reader is interested in beta reading, I sign him up to a dedicated list. The reader will automatically get the first message with the manuscript and my guidelines. Later on, I send a couple broadcasts to that list, reminding my beta readers about a deadline. I activate this list once again around the book's launch date, inviting them to get the book from Amazon and write a review.

When I organize my beta reading campaign this way, I save all the time it would take to write individual emails. More important, though, I save a ton of time that I would otherwise have had to spend on manual email management in my inbox. I send quite a lot of personalized messages to my beta readers anyway, but they are thank you notes to those who actually took action and contributed to improving the manuscript. If someone promised feedback but didn't deliver, he will only get automated autoresponder and broadcast messages.

In short, do use scripts. Even if you contact just five people, it will save you time. However, the fewer people you contact and the closer your relationships with them, the more work you should put into personalizing those scripts.

Remember:

- • If you can't see a win in the deal for whoever you're communicating with, you'd better refrain from sending the message altogether.
- • Read the draft of your message from the perspective of the receiver.
- • Use scripts to lessen your workload, but personalize your messages as much as possible.

Action Items:

- Reflect about why people would get benefit from connecting with you.
- List the attributes you bring.
- Today, communicate one of those attributes to someone. Even a beginner in any subject can bring this attribute: a willingness to comment on an individual's blog posts because of the value received from them. The blogger receives gratitude and feedback and an attentive audience. You receive good information that helps you.

11. IF YOU CAN'T CONNECT, MOVE ON

OK, you've found something to offer as their win, you've written a script, you've personalized it for each person separately, and sent your proposition to them... And nobody replied. What to do? You must follow up.

I heard an influencer say on a podcast that he purposefully doesn't reply to the first pitch he receives. He wants to check out how determined the other person is.

The fact that you haven't received an answer to your pitch doesn't necessarily mean it was rejected. There are a zillion possible reasons that someone didn't reply. From my experience people don't answer because they are overwhelmed, too busy, or simply don't know you well enough to bother. That's why it's so important to appear on their radar first.

There are some special circumstances when you shouldn't follow up, but not many. For example sending a second message about the same issue to the editor of a big site like Huffington Post or Entrepreneur is a faux pas, especially if they explicitly stated that they manage their emails with some delay and don't want to be bothered with additional correspondence.

But usually, you should follow up at least once. In many cases, more attempts may be futile and annoying for your eventual partner. But in cases where you've built awareness and exchanged a couple of tweets or comments, it may be worth sending them a few more emails.

On the other hand, what do you have to lose? If you've built awareness about yourself, exchanged a couple of tweets or comments, and yet the other party is ignoring you, there's not much you can lose by sending them a few more emails. You invested time and effort that you'll have wasted if you don't seriously try to entice some response. (Even if your eventual answer is "Get lost and don't bother me again," at least you will know where you stand). Recall the Bible parable of a widow and a corrupted judge: "I must give this widow her just rights since she keeps pestering me." (Luke 18: 5)

Let's assume you get some kind of answer. Should you follow up further? Your course depends on the context. Sometimes you've asked for a simple thing and they've agreed. There is no need to write again about this. Sometimes they'll ask for more details, or they'll invite you to a project of their own. Do yourself a favor: answer them.

Use your common sense and reply when it makes sense. Just remember that the last word doesn't have to be yours. Use this wonderful Arabian proverb to judge the validity of sending another message: *"The words of the tongue should have three gatekeepers: Is it true? Is it kind? Is it necessary?"* The words of your emails should have the same gatekeepers.

If you gave some kind of deadline in your pitch, the ideal moment to follow up is as the deadline approaches. If you invited them to join your book launch, it's totally sensible to send a reminder a couple of days before the launch date.

What to do in case of rejection? As another famous proverb says, "No means no." Unless you have a really great relationship with your partner, trying to change their mind is hopeless. You will waste your time and theirs, and the electrons used to send your email.

So, don't follow up. There is however one action you should consider: blacklisting them, especially if they were rude or didn't bother to personalize their reply. You've put in time and effort and proposed something beneficial for their audiences and they were indifferent. That doesn't seem like a recipe for a working relationship in the future.

Formal blacklisting is not necessary. If you are like most people, rejection hurts you, and you remember very well who has done it to you. The more stupid excuses I get, the ruder the reply, the better I remember the person. In the beginning of 2013, I submitted a guest post for an online contest. I did it more for fun than anything else, but I was pleasantly surprised when the staff member replied that, although my post wasn't suitable for the contest, they were interested in publishing it on their site. We had sent the post back and forth, ruthlessly editing it. The publishing date was set. I started to brag about it. Then, a few days before the publication date, they told me that my post had been rejected because "it doesn't have enough educational content, and reads too much like a rant." I was angry.

Heck, couldn't they have said that at the very beginning?!

By the way, this is a good reason to reject the pitches you receive politely and to the point. I considered the owner of that blog a nice guy. Not after that. I stopped visiting his blog and never recommended his stuff to anyone again.

Promises

"Smart people only believe half of what they hear. Wise people know which half to believe."

Apparently, I'm not smart nor wise. I don't know about you, but when someone doesn't keep his promises to me, it upsets me. That's why I was so angry with the blogger I mentioned above. Sometimes life just happens and you are not able to fulfill your promise or meet your deadlines. Inform your partners about that. Send a message, apologize, explain yourself (don't mistake an explanation for an "excuse") and propose some kind of compensation. Never ever leave the situation unexplained.

If you've promised something, always keep your part of the bargain.

Broken promises leave a really bad taste in one's mouth. If anyone does this to me, I usually give them another chance. I'm not a good Christian, I know; I should do it 77 times.

You should also be aware of your debt to the other person. We all have a keen sense telling us if we've been treated fairly, unfairly, or exceptionally. If you are in such a debt, I strongly recommend you follow up. This doesn't necessarily mean sending a message, although showing appreciation is always a good idea. You should pay off your debt with your deeds: try to provide even more value to your partner and his audience. Usually it will be enough to do more of what you did to get noticed in the first place: share their content, comment on their entries, and answer their calls to action.

Remember:

- Don't follow up only if the individual you're attempting to contact explicitly asked for a single message.
- There is a zillion possible reasons why someone doesn't answer. You should follow up at least once.
- "No means no." Don't waste your time on convincing when rejected.
- If you receive pitches yourself, and reject them, do it politely and to the point.
- Keep your promises. If you break one, don't leave the situation unexplained.

Action Items:

- Reflect on the times you've been rejected.
- What can you learn from these rejections?
- How will you make you next contact attempt differently?

12. VALUE YOUR JUDGMENT WHEN DECIDING WHO TO FRIEND

I've hinted at this a few times throughout the pages of this book: you should approach every contact with open eyes. Your goal is not to make as many relationships as possible in the shortest amount of time. Rather, your goal is to create valuable and sustainable bonds with others. To do that, you must be aware of your actions and efforts, but you must also scrutinize your current and potential allies.

The Bible says we should not judge each other. That's an ideal situation. Unfortunately, we are not ideal. In reality, we judge all the time, often judging instinctively. We subconsciously record all the intangible exchanges of social value between everyone around us, and we judge them by what we consider fair. Of course, we are all egocentric, and a huge number of misunderstandings result from individual perspectives of "fair." The idea with online networking is to replace this subconscious mechanism with at least rudimentary conscious "rules of engagement." Instead of using just feelings, use your brain from time to time.

I internally measure if the other person reciprocates in at least an even way. The simple Jim Rohn idea is my yardstick:

"Fool me once, that's not nice. Fool me twice, shame on you. Fool me three, shame on me."

When I notice that a relationship is taking an undesired course, that I'm contributing much more (or solely), I may decide to either withdraw my commitment entirely, or to became a "non-profit" contributor in the relationship. If I decide to call the relationship "non-profit," my engagement will significantly decrease. I will contribute only when it is suitable for me. No extra mile, sorry.

I'll give you an example: I once left a review on a book I'd read. The author sent me a thank you email and said that she would do a favor for me if I needed one. I asked her once, twice and got no reply at all. I'll never reach out to her again. I have enough troubles with promises I don't keep myself to want to introduce into my social circle people who are even worse than me in that regard.

What criteria should you use? Your own of course. Everybody has his own expectations and may be faced with different levels of relationship with each new person. Apart from "fool me" rules, I have a variety of criteria I use in online interactions.

Take Twitter for example. So far, I have been able to superficially scrutinize every follower and I have clearly defined criteria about whether to follow them back.

1. If I've interacted with the person earlier on some other platform, I immediately follow back.

2. If I find in their profile description a get-rich-quick scheme, I immediately forget about this individual.

3. If someone shared my stuff, I take one glance at their profile and in 99.99% of cases, I follow them back. Because so very few people share my stuff, I value sharers highly.

4. If someone shares mainly mainstream media news and gossip, I don't follow back.

5. In general, I check out their profile, looking for signs of authenticity, and any value they can provide to me:

-do they share stuff relevant to me?

-do they reply to individual tweets?

-do they share something about their lives?

-do they want to sell me something or are they looking for a genuine connection?

I also have highly individual criteria, like if they are sharing only images. I find images on Twitter highly distracting, so in most cases I don't follow back a person who does that.

I have a different set of criteria for gurus. I understand they have thousands and thousands of followers and cannot physically reply to each and every person.

However, I don't follow them just to be dazzled by their glory. I don't need much, just a sign that they notice and/or recognize me. When I sent Darren Hardy a screenshot from the Amazon bestseller list where my book was next to his, he replied with "Love it!" It was enough for me to follow him.

When I shared on Twitter an episode of "Entrepreneur on Fire," John Lee Dumas very promptly replied to my tweet thanking me and asking for a review. I followed him and it was through his podcast that I met my mentor, Aaron Walker, for the first time.

At the beginning of my presence on Twitter, I was stoked each time a bigshot with a big following followed me (big for me was only 1,000 back then) and I automatically followed them back. But my goal on Twitter is not to impress others with the number of my followers. I want genuine connections or at least a potentially genuine connection. Now, when someone with 10,000+ followers follows me, I check to see if they are able to manage such a big community and are personal in their approach: I send them a tweet asking why they followed me. If they reply, I follow them back. If not, there is no sense in being another trophy follower for them. It's highly unlikely we will ever exchange a single message.

What if you don't have such criteria? Well, start working on them. When I registered on Twitter, I didn't have such elaborate "who to follow" rules. I learned the ropes, observed what worked and what didn't, determined my goals (Knowing your targets is important. How else can you achieve them?), and painstakingly worked out my rules.

I kept them all in my head until I began writing this book. This was a mistake. I should have written them out a long time ago. Be wise and don't repeat my mistake. When you get some enlightenment on how should you act, or react, on this or that social medium, jot it down. It will leave a sign in your memory more permanent than just a thought. It will install a filter in your brain. Next time you are on this medium, you will be more likely to act in a desirable way without a conscious effort to do so.

You don't have to start a separate file for such notes. Just write your idea down once, and it will be many times more powerful than a feeble thought going through your head. You will develop (and act in accordance with) your criteria much faster and you will be more efficient. (It took me almost two years to gather 500 Twitter followers).

Remember:

- Replace your subconscious judgment mechanism with some conscious 'rules of engagement.' These can be rudimentary, but writing down your intentions makes it more likely that you will act consistently.

Action Items:

- Design your own criteria for online social media interactions.
- Commit your criteria to paper, or record it in an online file that is easily accessible.

13. OTHERS WILL JUDGE YOU, AND THAT'S A GOOD THING

Why should you care so much about who is in your audience and who follows you? A couple of reasons:

1. You want more than an illusion of grandeur.

The quantity of your followers doesn't count nearly as much as their quality. Once you have 100, 300, 500 or 1000 people on your email list, or following you on Twitter, you'll start to think that you are the man (woman ;)). But the reality is different.

Right now I have over 700 people on my email list. Not too bad, right? Wrong. Only about 180 of them open my emails. This is the number that really counts. If people don't even read my messages, they may as well be dead or living in a different galaxy. I don't have access to them; I can't communicate with them.

2. This one is of utmost importance: you will be judged by the people you associate with.

Think about it. How many times have you been open to a new acquaintance because you were introduced by a friend? How many times were you wary about some person because someone you have a low opinion about was talking them up?

When I am introduced to someone, especially online, my default approach is wariness... unless he or she is being introduced by a friend. It doesn't excuse me from forming my own opinion, but it gives the person being introduced a chance she wouldn't have had otherwise. Even if I'm skeptical about someone, a personal recommendation makes me reach out and try to form a relationship. I use my friend's social lenses and suspend (at least initially) my own judgment.

It doesn't mean that the success of such new relationships can be taken for granted. Remember the author who promised me a favor and then ignored me? I was introduced to her by my mentor. I know they have a good relationship. They even wrote a book together. But, once introduced, she failed to follow my (internal, unannounced) rules, so I don't intend to spend any more time on this relationship.

The negative impression works a bit different for me. When someone I don't respect or trust tries to introduce someone new to me, I disregard their recommendation. I treat the new lead as a stranger who needs to go through my normal "firewall."

On the other hand, if a friend warns me against someone, I won't generally even bother verifying them. I'll trust my friend and avoid that person.

Your reputation will depend on who you associate with. You may argue that this is unfair, that you are who you are. You may think you shouldn't be judged in this way by your friends and colleagues, as such judgment is stupid and superficial.

Here's another viewpoint. You really are the average of the five people you spend the most time with. Human beings are natural sponges. This is a totally subconscious mechanism that we use to cope with life. It is how babies learn: they observe people around them and mimic them. If your friends are jerks, you are most probably a jerk too. If they are saints, you may be one too. You can't help but become like those you closely associate with.

Don't be offended by this conclusion. Being angry about reality doesn't change it. Armed with this knowledge, be mindful about those you allow into your social circle. Consciously seek relationships with people you want to emulate. Consider who you want to become, and what character qualities you want to possess. Then associate with people who already have these.

Don't set different rules for people online and offline. Be congruent and keep in mind that you want real people to interact with, not more zeros next to your social profiles.

Remember:

- The quality of your followers does count much more than their quantity.
- Your reputation will depend on who you associate with.
- Don't set different rules for people online and offline.

Action Items:

- At the end of the last chapter, you designed some rules for yourself to use when assessing new social media contacts. Now design your own criteria for online interactions with individuals you deliberately approach or have recommended to you.
- Commit your criteria to paper, or record it in an online file that is easily accessible.

14. NETWORK; YOU'VE NOTHING TO LOSE

See? I didn't lie when I suggested that successful networking is straightforward; it doesn't involve complex half-magical stuff. Networking is something you, and everyone else, are naturally inclined to do.

Now go and network. What have you got to lose? Time? Time will pass anyway. Whatever you do with it, whether you play a computer game or start following a bunch of bloggers in the hope of connecting with them, your time will be lost.

You have nothing to lose. Even if you are ignored (which happens from time to time) you will learn something new. To connect with people you need to know them better, consume their content. This process alone will allow you to grow. Sometimes you will be rejected, but with rejection always comes a lesson you can learn from. If you take action, you will always receive some feedback. Action always incites reaction. Each interaction, no matter what the final outcome, means some feedback that you can digest and use as fuel for your growth.

Act; you can only profit from it.

You have a lot to gain. You can get whatever you ask for (ask and you shall receive) and so much more. Mind you, people are the most unpredictable factor in this world. We can understand the mechanisms of physics, but we are not even close to comprehending the complex dynamics of an individual's personality and society as a whole.

Usually we associate unpredictability with danger. This isn't right at all. Surprises are shortcuts to change. I didn't expect that marketing specialist Chris Bell would propose creating a book launch for me. Initially we agreed only upon the editing. His input into *Master Your Time*'s launch has forever changed the way I operate. First of all, his input caused the launch to be more successful than anything I had undertaken before. My book has sold over 4,000 copies since publishing, about 1,000 of them in the first month. It expanded my belief about what's possible and achievable.

I didn't expect to be approached by a publisher, no matter how small it was. When Matt Stone from Archangel Ink made me a proposal, I was hesitant and doubtful. Rightfully so. They overpromised. But from our cooperation over a few months, I got a big takeaway: publishing is a business and I need to invest in it.

I published my first book paying just $5. Now I'm preparing the launch of the first (and always free) part of *Six Simple Steps to Success*. I spent $275 just for the eBook version. I will never earn more than $10 from this book, but I invested almost $300 to publish it. I know now that the real benefits are down the road: more people will check out the free material and buy other parts of the series. More people will sign up to my mailing list, so I will get more chances to interact with them and improve their lives.

The surprises you get as the result of the influence of other people are most valuable. Without my cooperation with Archangel Ink, I wouldn't have learned my investing lesson. I invested about $3,000 in my business in 2015. I earned three times as much in royalties. Much more significantly, I influenced my readers' lives. I got the chance to affect thousands of lives, not merely hundreds.

But let's assume that you try to reach out to others and absolutely nothing comes of it. Nobody will do a single thing you've asked them for. You are ignored or derided. It cannot be beneficial in any way, can it?

I believe action is never fruitless. In the worst case, your takeaway is experience. You may not get your books reviewed or your project presented to potential partners' audiences, but you will always gain experience and experience always matters. If you can amass 10,000 hours in any venture, you will become an expert. Mind you, I didn't instance 3,000 hours or 8,452 hours. If you give up in the middle (or even near the end) of collecting your lessons, you will be knowledgeable at best (and a loser at worst). Experience, like everything in the world, compounds. If you cash in too soon, your "profits" will be only a fraction of what they could have been if allowed a few more years.

Get rid of your instant gratification mindset. It's an illusion. Nothing is instant in this world (except maybe instant coffee, but is that stuff really coffee?). The most valuable things are built with time: muscles, relationships, children, enterprises.

So, if you have no results, if you are not a master networker yet, just keep going. Your experience will be profitable in the end. You always learn in the process. You never start as a great player. You have to learn the ropes first.

While developing my publishing career I made a lot of errors. I lost a lot of money and time. I bought products and services I didn't need (not many of them, because I'm a Scrooge by nature). But this learning curve profited me down the road. A few months ago a "new" promo book site contacted me. They offered an attractive deal: they guaranteed 10,000 free downloads of my book for just $100. I couldn't put my finger on what exactly was wrong with this offer. I did some research and discovered that their site is new, so they couldn't have any experience or a big following of their own.

The authors' names on their testimonials were completely foreign to me. In the end I used the ultimate discerning tool: I contacted them. I learned that when in doubt, this is the best way to discover the real intentions of the other side.

They didn't reply at all.

A few weeks later they were revealed as scammers in the authors group I'm in. Yes, they were providing downloads and affecting Amazon's algorithms, but they were doing that by creating thousands of phony Amazon accounts. Authors told the stories of their buddies who had used that service and had their publishing accounts shut down for weeks by Amazon.

Because of my previous "failures," I was able to avoid that particular trap. Having my account shut down for a few weeks could have cost me as much as $1,500 if it had happened at the "right" moment.

Learning networking is like learning any other skill. You won't be any good at the beginning. You will get meager results initially. But those first lessons will be the most valuable, allowing you to improve your technique so you are better next time.

When I was launching *Master Your Time* at the beginning of 2014, I sent something like two dozen "cold" emails. I learned my lesson. I don't do that anymore. It's not worth the results. It's much better to warm up the relationship and then ask for a favor. The results are significantly greater and I gained a valuable additional reward—the relationships themselves.

Remember:

- Whether you make more contacts today, or tomorrow, or not, time will pass anyway.
- When you reach out with a service-orientated viewpoint, the people you reach out to will get something from the interaction and are more likely to become worthwhile contacts.

Action Items:

- Reflect about who your "ideal" business contacts are, and what the benefits to you would be, if you could get on their radar.
- Make a plan to contact one of these people this week. You now know that this is as simple as sending feedback about something you've read. But there are many ways.
- What are you going to *do?*

15. IT'S YOUR TURN

Connecting is easy. If I, a hardcore introvert, can do this, anyone can. We are group animals. It is natural for us to establish and cultivate relationships. New means of communication haven't changed that. In fact, they have facilitated the process. Everything you've heard from the media about how hard it is to maintain a stable relationship in the modern world is bollocks. The critics have cherry-picked the worst cases because those stories sell best. In reality, people are as hungry for meaningful relationships as they always were (maybe even more).

No, I'm not interested in reading your book if I've never heard about you and you've never provided some value to me. Yes, I would love to read it if you are my reader/ fan/ subscriber who has interacted with me in the past. It's as simple as that.

While interacting in an online world, don't give in to the temptation of pretending to be someone else. It's very draining mentally when you have to keep track of lies and half-truths you've spread around. Be yourself. Act with integrity and transparency. Pretending never works in the long run. Human internal BS radars are too sensitive to stay tricked for an extended period of time. You will gain trust and the commitment of your partners much faster, and your relationships will be more stable, if you just be yourself.

Genuineness is the most important factor you can exhibit. In second place is consistency. It's really hard to impress those folks who are above you. You just don't have what it takes yet. You are in the position of penitent; you need something from them. One-time brilliant action that provides some value to them is beyond your capabilities. However, you can do small things and you can do them consistently. Share their stuff, comment on their posts, cheer them up. Everything matters. You not only appear on their radar, you will be marked in their memory. Quite recently, I asked Steve Scott for a Skype call, just like that, out of the blue. He agreed and wrote:

"I know we've exchanged multiple emails and you've always been very

supportive."

Man! *I* was supportive? When Scott sent an email to his list, my book became a bestseller. A few months later he mentioned another of my books on his Facebook profile; it received a few hundred downloads. In January 2015 he did that with yet another book, which became a bestseller too. These three direct actions helped me immensely, but so did his teaching about self-publishing, which I sucked up like a sponge. This indirect guidance contributed greatly to my success. But he thinks *I* have been supportive!

What have I done for him? I've sent him a few encouraging messages and acknowledgments. I wrote a blog post about his book on my blog, which gets just a pitiful trickle of visitors. I commented on about 90% of the posts on his blog. I retweeted his tweets. I replied to several calls to action in his newsletter and on social media. It was nothing fancy. I couldn't do more. I was too small. What I couldn't do in weight I made up for in consistency.

Here is another example of consistency in action: I followed the blog of a millionaire. This blog was a new venture of his; he earned his fortune offline, so had no big online following. I commented on every single post of his. While reading one of my replies, he got concerned about me and sent me an email with his phone number saying he wanted to talk with me. Am-A-Zing.

Those kinds of opportunities are born out of consistency.

Design your game plan. Choose your own criteria. Who do you want to connect with? If you have some big names in the back of your mind, that's fine, you can jot them down, but don't start with those. Ponder why you want to connect with them, rather than someone else. Which of their qualities or deeds has stirred your interest?

You have to act in support of your own values. It is the only course of action that is sustainable. I've provided a lot of examples and my "whys" in this book, so I hope you now know what to look for. Just to recap, when I purposefully follow someone, I do it based on my two main criteria: I admire their character and they are approachable. Those two things combined are the green light for me. What's the use of following even the best guy in the world, when I could never exchange a single message with him?

Don't aim just for numbers. Following people with audiences

numbered in the millions will, in reality, diminish your chances for any meaningful interactions. When deciding who to build relationships with, pay attention to whether they engage their followers on a one-to-one basis. Jeremy Frandsen and Jason van Orden from Internet Business Mastery have tens of thousands of followers on Twitter, but they both reply to messages. I prefer to choose people who are slightly less known and grow through real interactions. I value authenticity and attention to people, and I follow "gurus" who demonstrate those values.

All successful people emphasize the importance of creating meaningful relationships. Spend as much time on networking as you are able to. And don't do it in spurts, either. Incorporate your networking practices into your life and schedule. Do as much as you can, but no more. With my full-time job, I can read and comment on a couple of posts or articles a day, and listen to two or three podcast episodes a week. This is the pace I can maintain in the long run. This is not impressive, is it? But in a year I listen to 100–150 podcast episodes and read 700 posts. Even small activities compound.

Sustainability is important because it begets consistency. Relationships need cultivation. A one-time event is not enough to create a relationship and it is definitely not enough to keep one alive. Consistency provides what in marketing jargon is called "impressions." The more we are bombarded with marketing messages, the longer it takes us to decide to purchase something. I read that nowadays a brand or product needs to appear in front of a customer's eyes 27 times before he will take some action. Your consistency will create "impressions" in the minds of the people you will follow. They can ignore you once, even 5 times, but after 27 interactions… I assure you, they WILL notice you.

Relationships are not something to play with or abuse. You don't create them to drive your agenda. The ultimate goal of every connection you make should be friendship. If you use the tips I've provided in this book simply to close a deal, to have your book featured on some blog or your online course promoted to someone's email list, and then cut off the connection, your "technique" will backfire. People will notice and word will spread. This is a small world and it's getting smaller each day. Sooner or later you will be revealed as a fake.

Once you decide to build a relationship, consider it for life. I see only one reason to give up on the connections I make and withdraw my commitment: because people change. If your partner chooses the Dark Side, if his values are no longer compatible with yours, you are justified in abandoning him.

Maybe lifelong commitment scares you a bit. Doing the same thing for the rest of your life sounds boring, doesn't it? Well, people are anything but boring. Keep in touch and you'll never be able to predict the outcomes.

If you invest your time and resources to create a relationship, but you don't see results, stop and evaluate. There are only two possible causes. The first is that your initial estimation of your partner was wrong. He or she is simply a jerk who doesn't care. But do you remember the internal BS radars we have? This option is not likely.

More probably you're just expecting results too soon. Instant gratification is a curse, doubly so in the case of lifelong commitments. You just haven't been providing value long enough. And you may have been doing it wrong, trying to push your agenda, instead on focusing on the other party. In any of those cases, a moment of reflection is a good idea.

Connecting is easy. It's easy for you. Embrace that thought. Now go and make some more connections in this amazing world of ours where everybody can reach out and touch the lives of someone thousands of miles away.

In Summary:

Networking is no more difficult than the communicating you do every day to people you already know—because that is all networking is; it is talking to people. Networking with people you haven't yet got to know is only hard in your mind. Networking with the right attitude will not only prove easy, it will invigorate you.

But you'll have to dive in if you want to get wet!

Strangers have been described as friends we haven't met yet. Think about what you'd be willing to offer a stranger who you didn't expect anything from in return. Most of us will give a kind word without feeling we need to be "paid back". But people will help you if you help them; even if it's just to show their gratitude

Action Items:

- Think about those whose network you'd like to be in.
- Consider what you'd do for them, to gain that access. I've shown you many no-or-low cost ways you can give value to almost anyone.

  My challenge to you is this: Pick one and do it today. And then write and let me know how it went—and what you learned from doing it.

< < < < The End > > > >

CONNECT WITH MICHAL

Thanks for reading all the way to the end. If you made it this far, you must have liked it! I really appreciate having people all over the world take interest in the thoughts, ideas, research, and words that I share in my books. I appreciate it so much that I invite you to visit www.ExpandBeyondYourself.com, where you can register to receive all of my future releases absolutely free.

Read a manifesto on my blog and if it clicks with you, there is a sign-up form at the bottom of the page, so we can stay connected.

Once again, that's

www.ExpandBeyondYourself.com

More Books by Michal Stawicki

You can find more books by Michal at:

http://www.ExpandBeyondYourself.com/about/my-books/

A Small Favor

I want to ask a favor of you. If you have found value in this book, please take a moment and share your opinion with the world. Just let me know what you learned and how it affected you in a positive way. Your reviews help me to positively change the lives of others. Thank you!

About the Author

I'm Michal Stawicki and I live in Poland, Europe. I've been married for over fifteen years and am the father of two boys and one girl. I work full time in the IT industry, and recently, I've become an author. My passions are transparency, integrity, and progress.

In August 2012, I read a book called *The Slight Edge* by Jeff Olson. It took me a whole month to start implementing ideas from this book. That led me to reading numerous other books on personal development, some effective, some not so much. I took a look at myself and decided this was one person who could surely use some development.

In November of 2012, I created my personal mission statement; I consider it the real starting point of my progress. Over several months' time, I applied numerous self-help concepts and started building inspiring results: I lost some weight, greatly increased my savings, built new skills, and got rid of bad habits while developing better ones.

I'm very pragmatic, a down-to-earth person. I favor utilitarian, bottom-line results over pure artistry. Despite the ridiculous language, however, I found there is value in the "hokey-pokey visualization" stuff and I now see it as my mission to share what I have learned.

My books are not abstract. I avoid going mystical as much as possible. I don't believe that pure theory is what we need in order to change our lives; the Internet age has proven this quite clearly. What you will find in my books are:

- Detailed techniques and methods describing how you can improve your skills and drive results in specific areas of your life

- Real life examples

- Personal stories

So, whether you are completely new to personal development or have been crazy about the Law of Attraction for years, if you are looking for concrete strategies, you will find them in my books. My writing shows that I am a relatable, ordinary guy and not some ivory tower guru.

Recommended books:

- *How to Work a Room* by Susan RoAne

- *You are a Writer* by Jeff Goins

- *How to Win Friends and Influence People* by Dale Carnegie

- *Will the Real You Show Up?* by Kim Garst

Made in the USA
Columbia, SC
29 October 2018